The Beginner's Guide to Minor Gods & Other Small Spirits

Kimberly Ramos

Acknowledgements

"I Think I Would Be Better," *Windfall*

"consider the salmon," *West Trade Review*

"a window overtaken by ivy," *Whale Road Review*

"Folklore for Missouri Boys," *Plainsongs Magazine*

"Dentures," *Underground*

"Basement," The *Lindenwood Review*

"cut in the earth," *Southern Humanities Review*

"Face Mites," *Windfall*

"Brain Teaser," *Bluestem Magazine*

"Julienne," *Road Runner Review*

"something small," *Arc Magazine*

"If You Came to Visit," *Windfall*

"Different Kinds of Sky," *Windfall*

"Essay as an Aporia," *Jet Fuel Review*

"Rover," *Windfall*

"Yahoo Answers," *Windfall*

"Ode to Graffiti," *Watershed Review*

"We Wake Up and Go Looking," *Mineral Area Council On the Arts*

Table of Contents

I. FINS & LEAVES

I Think I Would Be Better   8

How To Catch a Person with Your Lips   10

morning glories   11

consider the salmon   12

Love Letter with Crustaceans   13

girl from the lagoon   14

Mimicry   16

a window overtaken by ivy   18

Drosophila Melanogaster   20

Folklore for Missouri Boys   22

II. BONES & BODIES

Ours is a Place   26

Dentures   28

Basement   31

cut in the earth   34

Face Mites   36

Julienne   38

Brain Teaser   40

Short Film   41

something small   45

If You Came to Visit   46

III. GODS & GRAVITY

Different Kinds of Sky: A Field Guide   50

Essay as an Aporia   53

   (After Sumita Chakraborty's Essay on Joy)   53

Rover   55

Eight Ways of Looking at the Moon   57

Yahoo Answers   61

Include at Least One Bold Lie   63

Ode to Graffiti   65

Socrates Goes to a House Party   67

Tin Can to God   69

housework   70

We Wake Up and Go Looking   71

I. *FINS & LEAVES*

I Think I Would Be Better

as a minnow,
a bullet body glinting
silver, brain a benign bundle of cells
crushed in the corner
of my skull.
The whole world inverted, the sky
an unreachable ocean,
I would flit between two shallow edges
of a muddy pond,
encounter nothing
but hazy shapes and staggered light.
Let me leave
my head, humid and heavy as a giant.
Let me be the length
of my pinky finger, fluorescent
in the late-afternoon sun,
only asked to eat algae, and then

one day be eaten,

a tangle of enzymes in acid.

Only asked to glimmer

for children who venture to the creek,

and twinge, jewel-like,

when they shriek,

oh, look, a minnow.

How To Catch a Person with Your Lips

Let a word hang silver from the corner
of your mouth.
Hook your fingers in theirs
and pull forward, slowly.
Offer the head of a beetle,
the syllable from your throat,
other lures
that sink and glimmer.
Be patient and do not disturb the water.
Look for movements
that are tender and full of turmoil.
Let the line run taut in your hands
and be a gentle sort of stubborn.
Now eat or release:
the bones of a beautiful thing
or scales flashing in a river.

morning glories

we never planted the morning glories / but still / they came every spring / and wound around / the poles meant for the bean plants / vines twining / in infinite spirals / my father said they would get out of hand in a hurry / if we were not careful / so we would unwind them / slowly, in early morning / when they opened sweetly / to drowsy bees / and hurried hummingbirds / their violet skins bursting forth / breathing blue / breathing love / as a child, i thought it a shame / to hate / these soft skinned hands / these brightly smiling fans / but my father was adamant / about freeing up the space / for the other plants / i did not understand / until today / when i found you / curling around my bones / vines along my thighs / femurs of flowers / a sea of green / rupturing between / my sun-bleached ribs / my ears spilling / your silken songs / your petaled words / opening / closing / my heart a bloom / opening / closing / a thing i did not intend / but now must tend to / or cut at the root / but oh, i find bare bones / so boring / if steepling my fingers / into a trellis of flesh / meant you would cover me / i would hold so still / until i curved inwards from the weight / of your veins and blossoms / dew drop fresh / moving / to catch the sun

consider the salmon

the salmon leaves the ocean / for the place upstream / where it
came into being / this is called / chemical memory / this is baked
/ in the bones / all this to die shortly after spawning / so
consider: / i throw myself up waterfalls / without fully knowing
why / scales spitting / light like prisms / the whole body arced
and airborne / i'm pulled to places / i dream-remember / swept
up in mouths / that feel familiar / when the salmon dies / it's a
form of politeness / making room for more mouths / more
decay / a rock growing ever smoother beneath / burgeoning
tides / nothing to hold on to / i want to obliterate every egg /
before it can lust after freshwater / to break a circle, you must
eat it / monstrous / but necessary / but imagine / all the beauty
i lose / in loving nothing / rainbowed scales / thick and fast in a
moving river / the cold gasp / of my body against a current /
closer and closer / to that first love

Love Letter with Crustaceans

Here, my spine.
Here, my carapace,
taut with chitinous skin.
Here, where you bore into my back
and removed all the soft innards
and showed me they were silken, crimson,
slick and watery fabric that melted in my hands.

Here, a memory:
luxury slipping through my fingers,
a salt song crackling on the radio,
intestine scarf flapping from the window—
your teeth sharp, but gentle.
All good things must be broken into:
eggs, crabs, bones—
yellow yolk, white meat, warm marrow.

girl from the lagoon

i.

the days leak from the corners of my mouth. it's all sludge,
time passing. i used to mark the hour by how much the trees
gossiped when i left your house, by how much warmth the
concrete stole out of me on the way back home.

ii.

yes, this is a form of self-indulgence. yes, this is my sick sort of
joy: wishing worlds into existence. world in which i breathe
leaves into my lungs, world in which i shower at your place,
world in which yes, yes i do want it.

iii.

quickly and painlessly i fall into bed. i've been weaving grass
through my teeth, tempting moths and other delicate husks. i
stuff my ears full of honeysuckle, call it a sweet nothing.

iv.

feet half-dragging, i hover over the swamp. i've got a pear for a heart and two yellow eyes. i'm becoming beautiful, and what are you going to do about it?

v.

i like things best when they just barely graze my fingers, then slip away. silken and dreaming. every flower caught in the bog feels like it's from you.

vi.

last week i saw you in the gaps between other bodies, and my chest swelled with your voice. my eyes barely above the water, i'm begging: don't tell anyone i have gills.

vii.

tell me that you hear me, that somewhere i'm making ripples in the water, that yes, yes the moon reminds you a little bit of me, that your thumb is still painted black in my name.

Mimicry

So much of what I am is borrowed,
stolen, stapled together.
Am I a beetle
dreaming she is a girl,
or a girl dreaming she is a beetle?
Everyone knows
but me.

If I grind my teeth,
does that mean I am hungry?
And I have eaten
so much already:
rubber tires, open wounds, my own
fingers. I am a little afraid

of mirrors, and that includes the one
nestled in the back

of your throat.
I don't know how to push light
out of me, but everyone else
makes it seem easy,

gathering up every photon
they ever swallowed
and parceling them out as gifts.
Instead, I diagram desire
as if it were a science—
the exchange rate of bones to flowers

is two knuckles for three orchids.
I catch moths
and hold them in my fists
before offering you their broken wings.
It is so hard to be the right kind of gentle,
to hold anything without ripping it apart.

Somewhere, celestial bodies chart their course.
They know exactly when to touch.

a window overtaken by ivy

once a summer, my mother / had to remove the ivy / from the
siding of our house / to keep it from overtaking the windows /
and shrouding the family pictures, the fireplace, the couch / in
green shadows / i mourned the loss / the thin tendrils ripped
from the bricks / leaving dried veins as a memory / of the
leaves that climbed / twisted / finagled their way inside / this
was the first time i learned / that a beautiful thing could kill
you / but every season / the ivy grew back / slick and stubborn
/ green fingers gripping the bricks / we never noticed it / until
the ivy was / a beard of leaves mocking us / lush / a life
overtaking our lives / daring us to kill it / grinning and ripping
/ chunks of our house away with it / my mother tried fire /
tried poison / tried knives / still the ivy rose again / quiet as
smoke / the silent creeper / tapped at my window / romeo,
romeo / i let it in / and let it kiss me / overwhelm me / the ivy
climbed my spine / crawled into my skull / brain burdened,
heavy-headed / i rested all summer / slept as ivy crept / across
my eyes / between my teeth / out of my nose / mouth of ivy /
palms of ivy / brain a ball of ivy / japanese beetles shuddered
beneath my leaves / dotted ladybugs / soft and hollow moths /
the grief of greenery / when i spoke / there was the sound of
leaves rustling / my bones crumbled / my fingers broke off /
my limbs stiff and decrepit / my body an ivory ruin / shattered

windows / from when kids broke in / ivy trailed the floors /
looped across the ceiling / carpet of ivy / chair of ivy / lamp of
ivy / organs of ivy / my mother found me sleeping / in a bed
of ivy / with gothic spires for fingers / mold in my molars / i, a
moss-ridden moth house / she could not pull the ivy off /
without pulling me apart / i, a little juliet sleeping / she could
not wake me

Drosophila Melanogaster

My friend, the biologist,
tells me there are many different ways
to kill a fruit fly:

by drowning, by ether, by apple cider vinegar;
many small bodies floating
in a golden graveyard.

She can deftly uproot brains, whole nervous systems
with a flick of her tweezers.
She takes apart hearts, disassembles genes,

gracefully peels off wings.
It is not unkind, all this killing. It is nothing at all.
Most live little more than a month;

what is a few weeks less?
Mechanical, moving parts, thin limbs
crawling along the inside

of test tubes. Their patterns of flight
a thing of interest.
It must be like love, being observed

so closely and so faithfully. If we know anything,
it is that their insides are valuable,
little storehouses

of knowledge. Their children in the same service.
My friend, the biologist,
will donate her body to science. She clocks in,

moves in predictable paths through the lab,
a being of ether. She will hold
the living rapt even in death, give and give

of paper, of numbers,
of the steady lung thrum
and then, the hush of holding a human heart.

Folklore for Missouri Boys

Cut away the skin, bone, fat
of some dolphins washed ashore
and you'll find a boy nestled
in the slick, gray body.
Uncurling from sleep,
his eyes are as dark as a deep-sea vent.

We dress the boys in shirts and pants
and tell them how lucky
they are to have legs.
We send them into landlocked fields of grass
with hatchets and knives.
These boys, they only laugh when it rains.

These boys, they crouch low to watch
tadpoles at the creek, a sad hunger.
These boys, they long for salt and brine,

they fill their heads with water
and then they stumble home.
These boys, they kiss whoever's closest—

a body to rise against them like a tide,
its breath,
its fickleness,
and finally, after a storm: stillness.
These boys, they get married
and on weekends, they go fishing.

They bait their hooks
with skin and nails
like the water
might remember them,
like every sewer might be a way
back to the ocean.

II. BONES & BODIES

Ours is a Place

Ours is a place for spelunking. I've had friends come back from Meramec, Fischer, Cliff, their eyes struck through with stalactites. They say: It's like being in a stomach, the sounds of digestion all around you. They say: I heard a large heart beating that far down. Must be why we call it the Heartland—and like a heart, we have stolen it, the very name a scar carved into grade school history books. Once, in grade school, we found a dead armadillo in the bushes, were told not to touch it—but the bravest among us secretly skimmed its scaled skin. I remember this story every time I see roadkill, my license cutting like a knife in my pocket. By being I am killing. How many masses of matted fur have I condemned to the side of a highway? It is hard to say. These days, I clamber in and out of mouths, flashlight in hand. I wrestle sentences out of back molars, save syllables from slipping down throats. All these canaries gone silent in lead mines. Once, I found a yellow feather on my father's pillow, and I feared for his life. Brave, I want to be brave. The Greeks laughed at a man with knives in his eyes, and though it did not make the abyss any less dark, it made it less unhomely. You see, it's quieter here. The fields, open. We are small people carving out small lives in the belly of a god. We are not so deluded so as not to hear the sounds of digestion all around us. Not enough neon to blind us: the stars wink out their sad predictions. Ours is a place best loved at night: the dark and humid air, the day not yet caved in, the whole world a bauble taken out of an infant's mouth.

Dentures

Everything else renews itself in a timely manner:

twenty-seven days for skin,

ten years for bones,

and an astounding five minutes

for the thin cells of the stomach.

But the incisors say you

should be more responsible,

rot graffitiing the back

of the bicuspids.

When I was five I had three crowns

for the three caverns that I acid

burnt with kool-aid, sugar sliding

down the back of my throat.

I ate mud pies, cracked pebbles in the back

of my jaw. Did ugly
things with my mastication maw,

dirty words for a dirty place
of crumbs and old saliva and now
when you say my teeth
are pretty and straight I can feel

the phantom pains of wire lies.
I scheduled a dentist appointment
on my own for the first time
and my molars moaned their thanks.

I brush so that I won't lose a front tooth again,
so that my mother won't have
another bag of jangling
teeth to keep in the basement

with all the other baby things.
Every time the sharpness counts out
my canines I feel the pointed
reminder of faulty

joints and connectors,
how night grinding takes off
layer after layer, atomic fragments flaking
on my tongue—

the metallic tang of blood,
my teeth falling
one by one.

Basement

I don't like to think of the boxes sitting in my parents' basement, and I really don't like to think of the boxes that belong to me, the shantytown of seashells, broken crayons, and lackluster mementoes fermenting below the living room. A thousand dead things curled between tattered memories (once I found a family of roaches holed up against my kindergarten art) and the slow creep of mold in cardboard corners. Last time I went down there I stepped on a doll's head, flattened it, put its eyes on two different planes. Later I found a strand of its flaxen hair stuck to my sole. There's dust so thick it could be snow, and dust is at least seventy percent human, so every inhalation is a revival of a self long dead. Bones renew every seven years, skin in twenty-seven days, but the brain is even faster. Every neuron is a bullet firing off into the dark, a series of Christmas lights crammed in a dented box and shifting into infinite shapes. You'll never see the same shape twice. If the mind is a stage, mine is decaying, the actors are aging, I should exit left, pursued by the bear from sophomore English class. "Every breath is the death of something I used to be," and I know this because I wrote it in a half-filled journal from seventh grade (my edgy phase) and I like to act like I've outgrown everything, like I don't drag eighty pounds of participation trophies and faded poster board reports, like the glass eyes of stuffed animals don't make my soul shudder with remorse. At a certain age, you get two choices: burn all your shit or bury yourself in it, and I don't know which is going to hurt more.

When my parents were twenty-eight, newly married, a flood rushed past all the floorboards, turned the basement into a bog, and they tried to save stuff, they did, they slogged down there in rainboots and pulled up waterlogged biology textbooks from when my father wanted to be a teacher instead of a doctor, they submerged their forearms in mud to unmoor my mother's baptismal dress, they set grade school report cards in front of fans to dry them out, the paper rippled and brittle. Over half they had to throw away, and they sat in their empty house, the basement disemboweled, and they held each other because they'd just lost twenty years of their life to rainwater and they wanted to make sure they were both still solid and breathing. But the flood didn't touch any of my things, not my old clothes, not the lock of hair saved from my first haircut, those were tucked up on the top shelf, because even back then I was taught to be a tiny hoarder. Now I watch for rain clouds with horror and hope weighing on my chest, as if one good disaster could redesign me entirely.

In Catholic school, I learned that blessed items must be buried or burned, not thrown away or desecrated by racoons. In Catholic school I also learned that clean slates always cost something. Here are the worksheets if you don't believe it. Will my five-year-old self hang me heartless when I purge her twenty drawings of the family cat? I don't want to ask. And someday the ticket stubs I'm collecting won't mean anything, and if I don't throw them out, someone else will, but god, I think they're lovely now. I just want to believe that the body is more than a box used for eighty years, that somewhere in the sublevel darkness I'll always exist, breathing mildew and fumbling for the light switch.

cut in the earth

i have come to dread / the digging / i have heard all the sayings / dig long enough and you'll reach / china / magma / dead dinosaurs / men and women come / for excavation / they take apart hearts / move aside guts / cut through peritoneum / they leave stakes and tags / here, the penny i swallowed as a child / here, the spider that crawled / down my throat / they tell me they can retrieve / my history easily / in layers of clay / and roots / here, a red line from crying / here, thick loam from a good year / i say, what do you see / they say, quiet i'm reading / they scan me for carbon / for cruelty / for dead creatures / they find bodies / on bodies / on bodies / the men and women that came before / seeking riches / digging ditches / the deeper you go / the more dangerous it gets / some wanted my gold teeth / my turquoise bones / the silvery backs of my eyes / others wanted to discover a new land / to make a map / of epidermis / dermis / subcutaneous fat / but i have been known and named before / bone breaker / bog brain / cold desert / fallen city / who knew i had / all of that in me / i am sorry / i do not mean to eat / indiscriminately / but i cannot tell the difference / between / tomb raiders and lovers / i open my jagged maw / i chew and swallow / i add knuckles and knees / to the dark earthy feast / i am the sinking grave / i am the hungry pit / i suck love to dust / i leave fields fallow / stop asking me / for a relic or a ruby / all

i hold / are cold bones / leathery souls / and the aching need /
to know / and be known

Face Mites

I'm about to ruin your day: you have face mites living in the
pores of your face. They look like worms, but it's worse—
they're arachnids. Like ticks. Or spiders. Burrowing into the
small indentations of your nose, the folds of your mouth.
Making a whole life out of the two greased-up weeks they're
granted. All that sebum you pried out of yourself, forced out
with drugstore charcoal and tape, they're feasting on what's
left, face down and bottoms up. At night, they roam the great
planes of your face, looking for love. While you dream of
someone who doesn't text anymore, they're making out with
their grippy little pincers. While you shift your sheets in sleep,
they're making vows that'll last a lifespan of fourteen days.
These unbidden roommates, these freeloaders, you can't kill
them. One, anything that burns them burns you. Two, they're
sort of sentimental. When you lived in the sheltered, watery
darkness, you were clean. Scientifically sterile. Then your
lungs inflated with a great, shuddering shock, and your
mother loomed over you. The hitchhikers hit the highways of
your soft skin. Your father said, She has my ears, her mom's
eyes, our face mites. You can trace the spiraled ribbons of their
scrounger genes back and back, track the passage of face mites
forever, over land, over water. And maybe you've traded these
segmented sycophants, too. Maybe in the warm lamplight

they crawled from one face to another. Maybe those crisp white sheets were teeming with unbidden, squirming reminders. Now quantify the amount of your body populated by something else, someone else.

Julienne

is a pretty word for cutting
lengthwise.
Knife against the wooden board,
it will go through anything
just to kiss the grained
surface.
I julienne the carrots, cucumbers,
radishes, then my own
finger.
There are many words
that can get you into trouble:
please and *yes*
the worst offenders.
If I cut through your voice enough,
it becomes a sliver
to pocket alongside all the others.
I am not sure what happy people do with all their time

except for counting down

to the next rapture—

at one point, I might have asked you,

please blooming in my throat.

Once a vegetable has been cut in this fashion,

we say it's been julienned.

Yes, you say from your pile of carrot sticks.

Brain Teaser

If only I could abstract you a bit more. If only you were a wallet photo, a string of code, a dream I forgot after waking. Like Magritte, I cover your face with different objects. Apples. Doves. Flying fish. Like Magritte, I understand a pipe is not a pipe. Hint: you are the pipe. Touch me. Do not touch me. Schrodinger's cat is both alive and dead as long as the box remains closed. Hint: you are the box. The heart is a lump of tangled legs and matted fur, whiskers trembling on the side of the highway. Red guts along white lines. The brain, like most other organs, never gets the privilege of sunlight. In all that darkness, electricity blooming blue fluorescence. The brain a moon jelly undulating in the thick fluids of the skull. Hint: you are the skull. Cracked open it spills riches, blue yolk sliding in clear viciousness. Beautiful but better left in its shell. The corner of the eye is where most illusions occur. Shadows. Movements. People. Even with the edge of my eye I know your shape. Hint: you are the eye. I gather up your limbs and eyes and buttons. I lay everything in rows, edge to edge. I walk the whole perimeter. I scan your hands for patterns. I line your lips with thumbtacks and red thread. It's sitting on my tongue, a reverse flower, petals sinking into themselves.

Short Film

Int. Restaurant - Evening

A restaurant at rush hour. Couples sit at candlelit tables, light
haloing the wooden surfaces. There are small smiles, furtive
glances, indistinct chatter. A hand finds a hand, a mouth finds
a mouth.

BONES AND PANIC, a woman in their twenties wearing red
lipstick, enters the restaurant and speaks to the maître d'. He
leads them to a table near the center of the restaurant.

MAÎTRE D'
Your table, madam.

Bones and Panic takes a seat. They smooth out their dress, a
chiffon ensemble that almost reaches the floor. They flip up
their menu and study the entrees.

41

When they set the menu back down, they startle. The KNIFE-EATER has appeared in the seat opposite them. He wears a dashing suit and a gleaming smile.

KNIFE-EATER
(casually)

So, where are you from?

BONES AND PANIC

A small town. Before that, the bottom of the ocean. Before that, a void.

KNIFE-EATER

Charming.

BONES AND PANIC

What is the worst thing you've done?

KNIFE-EATER

Something like this.

The Knife-Eater flits his hand across the table and seizes the knife set before Bones and Panic. He pushes the cutlery down his throat, then smiles winningly.

KNIFE EATER (Cont.)

So, what do you think?

BONES AND PANIC

(nauseous)

I think I am thirsty.

The Knife-Eater pushes his suddenly full glass of wine towards Bones and Panic. They drink.

KNIFE-EATER

Do you live near here?

BONES AND PANIC

Far enough that I am hard to follow.

The Knife-Eater reaches for the hand of Bones and Panic and smiles reassuringly.

KNIFE-EATER

When was the last time you were happy?

BONES AND PANIC

Before I had a body.

KNIFE-EATER

Hm? You look cold. Take this.

He rises from the table and wraps his arms around the shoulders of Bones and Panic. He smiles into their neck.

KNIFE-EATER

Do you mind if I take a sip?

BONES AND PANIC

(resigned)

Not at all.

He takes a slow bite into the neck of Bones and Panic. They slump against the table.

The Knife-Eater smiles wetly. He is charmed.

something small

terrifying to think i could be accountable / for anything / i
could snag a soul / with my ring finger / lock box a heart and
lungs / set off a series of explosions / brainstem blooming tulip
heads / my net good / will not be another hungry mouth /
another pair of hands / grasping for sky / no, i know / i'm
young mud / three-quarters dismal / sick soul / not blind nor
brave enough / to let a wound fester / with the hope of
growing roses / i will leave an empty space / i will leave no
sound / there will be such quiet / those who mourn me / will
be half in the ground //

but if you come / by accident / i will love you / so heavily / it
might crush your small lungs / i want to apologize / for what
you will inherit from me / : / brain bog / rickety fingers / high
tide in the stomach / and gulls, so many gulls / field after field
/ and a quick-moving longing / you will never escape / maybe
you will bring me out of myself / this body of bent wings /
and you the blue flower beside it / but this is too much / to
ask / of anyone / no matter / how soft / your crown not even
closed / before the world falls in

If You Came to Visit

I would show you around, take you to see the sights. Like any good date, I would take you to Walmart. Hands almost brushing, we would walk down the aisles. I might buy you a five dollar flower bouquet, or if I'm short on money, a dollar candy bar. We would bury our arms elbow deep in the movie bargain bin, unearth 2000s rom-coms and box office failures. You might find a copy of an old 80s movie—*Sixteen Candles*, maybe, or *Pretty in Pink*—and you'd huddle close to tell me what you remember of it. You would place your hand on the small of my back, and the gesture might be enough to convince me to kiss you in the parking lot, the humid air pressing down on us.

I would drive us the long way home. Past the high school, past the strip mall, past the water tower looming like a giant. In the red of the stoplights, we would be thin-lipped silhouettes. You would be playing music from your phone, a band I've never heard of. The throaty warble of your voice in the dark. *Let's take a detour*, I would say. Anything to keep you singing. I would take us on back roads, trees dense and telling secrets. *Have you heard of parking?* I would ask. The lightning bugs would rise out of the grass with bated breath. You'd reach for me, and I'd reach for you, and for once the sky would not shatter.

We would get home late. My mother would be on the couch asleep. An old habit from my high school years, she would wait until we were home to go upstairs. I would wake her, walk her to bed. You would sleep in the basement for decorum's sake. You would stare down the crucifix above the door before you descended, your palms hot and sweaty. The creak on the stairs thirty minutes later would be my tentative step. In this way, I would be a ghost: near you at night, gone by morning. You would know me best under a white sheet, half-awake.

I would take you to the important places. The large plastic frog in the lake whose eyes stare ominously from the water, the rest of him submerged. The field half a mile from my house where I used to steal Queen Anne's lace. I would drive you past my old Catholic school, tell you stories about uniforms and sins and thin blouses. I would take you to Steak 'n Shake, treat you to cheap pancakes and a sugar coma. I would not tell you, *This is where my prom date took me after we slow danced senior year*. I would not tell you, *This is where I hiked with a boy who I couldn't love enough*. I would not tell you of the recent past. I would pretend to have forgotten all the bodies behind me. I would let them drift in the muddy water of the creek behind my house. The night before you planned to leave, they would come to the windows, tap on the glass. They would tell me, *It is not so easy to stifle young history, to obliterate it with spit and a thumb*.

In the morning, I would drive you to the city. We would go to the art museum, float across the tiled floors. In front of *Judith and Holofernes*, I would kiss you. The security guard might see us, but he sees iterations of us every hour: young people sneaking hands into each other's pockets and leaning into each other. In the park, there would be no onlookers for the girl with the head of a girl in her lap. Here, we would be a common beast. I would take a swig of cold tea, pass the bottle on to you. *Joan, I would say, do you think it hurts being burned at the stake?* You would answer, *A little, but not as much if there is someone waiting for you on the other side.*

III. GODS & GRAVITY

Different Kinds of Sky: A Field Guide

i.

Here's sundown—the sky drips down like a hot wax.

ii.

Sailors seem to like red skies, but not in the morning. Some say this is an old wives' story. Current research suggests that it might actually be the sky that loves the sailors.

iii.

Organ skies are common in the Midwest. You can identify an organ sky by the shape of the innards strung through the air like unholy streamers. The characteristic rumble in the distance is a stomach searching for its lost parts.

iv.

Skies, unfortunately, are not distributed evenly. The sunsets really are better at the beach and in, say, Key West, but this should not discourage you from sunset hunting in your current locale.

v.

Fever skies were said to be extinct, but they have shown a resurgence in recent years. You can see a fever sky best at a highway gas station as you lean against your car. Keep your feet steady—fever skies are known for their dizzying properties.

vi.

While sky hunting is a lovely pastime, certain precautions are necessary. Do not go outside on clear nights, when stars are at their hungriest. Gravity may reverse. Many novice sky hunters have lost their lives to the gods and bears.

vii.

Contrary to popular belief, smoke-storm skies are not a dangerous omen. Rather, smoke-storm skies are a form of fortune. You should count yourself lucky to eat the lightning and hail.

viii.

Recently, many sky hunters have reported the presence of moon halos in night skies. While there is little official evidence to this phenomenon, it is worth asking the moon about it.

ix.

Skeptics of the field of sky hunting claim that sightings of the Wyeth Giant are no more than myth. While they are rare, there are several instances of Wyeth Giant sightings, though skeptics point out that these sightings are usually made by children. Children, however, are just as reliable as anything.

x.

The merits of sky hunting lie not in the scenery or the identification, but the silence. Sunrise—and the sky pools in the driveways.

Essay as an Aporia

(After Sumita Chakraborty's Essay on Joy)

A star is brightest when viewed from the corner of the eye. To see a god swimming in his indulgence one must not look directly at him, but somewhere off to the side. It's something about the design of the retina, that silvery nebula stuffed in the back of the socket. An eye, when dissected, yields many parts, all of which fit in a fist. Heidegger writes, *We are too late for the gods and too early for Being.* All light is old when it reaches the eye. All images that reach the eye have already dissolved. I put my hand in the light but the light has moved on. If light had eyes, it would see everything instantaneously. It would jump from the sun to my palm. This is true. This is physics. The gods are gone but maybe a holy bone still explodes in my eyes. Maybe a bit of a god's light still tumbles down the side of the mountain. A boy once told me lightning was inefficient in the way it cut and curled and arced. If he had designed lightning, it would hit the trees and roofs in a straight, vertical line. This, he said, is good design. The light through the window laughed at his empty hands. Heidegger writes, *To head toward a star—this only.* At night I sit in the grass and wish for gravity to dissolve and hurl me from earth's breast. I want to touch young light and hold a photon in my fist. I want to see a star swimming in its gods. A knife of lightning lodged in my eye. The gods are physics but maybe a boy still yields many parts. I am too early for forgetting and too late for looking. I am instantaneously inefficient. My path is not straight but a jagged arm holding the sky. A star is brightest when viewed from the corner of the eye.

Rover

How you have appeased us, little juggernaut,
how we have slung you into the sky
to collect silver-flecked moon rocks,
to bottle Jupiter's stormy skin,
to steal us Neptunian rings
and their chrome glow for our fingers.
Now you say you are homesick?
Your signals sadden us
when there is still a long list of things to send back—
the buckle of Orion's belt,
a red cup of dust,
long ribbons of nebula to string in our hair,
other astronomical fare.
Do the dark spaces between suns
make you lonely?
Listen, we are suffering, too—we miss you.
Every single day, we do.

Please try to imagine our pain,

and keep sending back your pretty findings.

You are lucky to be up there

amongst the whirling, whistling, gleaming things

while we wait hand in hand below,

expecting your shipment of streamers and stars

to spiral into our arms.

Eight Ways of Looking at the Moon

i. *Formation*

Some think the moon was born out
of a geological kiss between two mothers,
a clashing of lips.
Others think it built itself alongside
the earth, like a younger sister mimicking
an older sibling.
Or maybe it took one look at Earth
and decided to elope.

ii. *Lunar Maria*

Lake of Softness settled near my soles
and Marsh of Sleep between my brows.
Bay of Love and Bay of Roughness,
one in each hand.

Lake of Dreams along my sixth rib.
Sea of Serenity overlapping
waves with Sea of Crises.

iii. *Space*
The moon loves best
at a distance.

iv. *History*
Hit me hard enough
and I'll turn to volcanic glass, the impact
shattering my kneecaps.
All my old bruises turn orange,
fermented memories.
Upon discovery, the Apollo 17 astronauts
could not believe the color.

v. *Phases*
The moon is called a celestial body
even though it is pockmarked with scars,
covered in craters.
It is loved when it is a sleep-heavy sliver

and when it is a glistening eye.

Its ivory fingers reach into the water

and pull in the tides.

vi. *Gravity*

The moon is drawn to things larger than itself,

and it does not resent this desire.

vii. *Myth*

The moon is home to droves of silken rabbits.

The moon is a hologram hanging

in the sky, projected from deep beneath the earth.

The moon is a loving goddess.

The moon is a small white pill of lunacy.

The moon hears girls singing

and loves the slow curls of shower steam rising.

viii. *Thief*

I siphon off light from other bodies—

I don't have enough of it in me.

I was not born bioluminescent,

my dullness is inherent,

but when I touch light I make it

soft, silver, silent,

and in the perfect dusk I paint the leaves.

Yahoo Answers

My girlfriend hasn't kissed me, and we've been dating for three months. She says it's because she's not ready, but I think she might not actually be attracted to me? For reference I am a 6'2" man, she is an 80'5"-wide black chasm. For reference, I have blonde hair and brown eyes, she has a pool of night raging between two cliffs. For reference, I am approximately a seven point two on a good day, she is unquantifiable. Some other details: we met at a coffee shop. She was drinking a latte. I was bumming the free wifi. Well, by drinking a latte, I mean she was the sink. I mean, she drank the lattes that got messed up, the ones that nobody wanted. She let each cup of golden coffee swirl for a second, then destroyed the white swirls of a universe. I mean, I fell in love instantly. We just clicked, you know? I slipped her my number, by which I mean I scrawled it on a napkin and then threw it away. For the rest of the day, I waited for her to call me. I saw her in the endless sewers. I saw her in the dark tunnels of the subway. I saw her in the space between my couch and the wall. And then, she called. My heart was basically a dying star collapsing on itself. I answered after two rings. She said, You should probably buy something if you're going to use that store's wifi. I said, I love you. She said, Let's see a movie. We saw a movie—but we didn't see a movie. We sat in an empty movie theater with the lights off. We stared at the blank screen as it fluttered with a draft. She moved closer, but she didn't kiss me. I wanted to kiss her. She said, Not yet, it's not time yet. I still want to kiss her, though. We've been dating for three months. Any advice on how to get her to kiss me?

Include at Least One Bold Lie

You Won't Believe What the Moon Jelly Did Next.
Seven Tips for Removing the Briar Patches From Your Lungs.
Top Ten Lies You Told Your Mother
(You'll Be Shocked by Number Eight!) A Definitive List
of All the Boys You Kissed.
The Problem with Trusting Luna Moths to Keep
Your Secrets. Lose Your Head Fast
With This Weird Trick. Why You Should Date
More Girls. Why You Should
Date Less Girls. Eleven Signs of Hidden Curses
(Naps Are One of Them!)
Five Recipes for Hectic Weeknights
When Everything Is Going Wrong. How to Survive
the Second Coming.
Remember You in Second-Grade? This Is What
She Looks Like Now.
Stop Biting Your Nails and Find Love.

Twenty Most Dangerous

Boys You Will Ever Talk To. How to Kill

With Only Nail Clippers.

This Quiz Will Reveal the Next Precious Gemstone

You Should Eat.

Learn the Secret of Biting Off Your Own Hands:

It Will Change Your Life!

Ode to Graffiti

I.
I do not know who R.P. is, but sometime

in 1968 he stood at the same cement
I am standing and etched
his blocky initials into the stone,
and threw, I imagine, a middle fingered salute
to the man the monument was really for.

II.
Maybe last weekend she saw her boyfriend
kissing somebody else, so she sequestered herself in a stall,
and using the permanent marker
she brought from home because those weak-ass janitors
weren't going to erase it this time,
scrawled her declaration:
Cheryl S is a slut!

III.
M.M.U. and J.H.
or one without the other
sat here and thought about each other

(or just one, about the other).
A heart ensnares them in decades-old commemoration—
forever lasts however long the letters stay legible.

IV.
Someone's pulse tapped incessantly beneath their skin
as they wrote it, a tempo of you are alive you are
alive you are alive you are alive
you cannot die—
a big ol' Fuck emblazoned on the Catholic school

playground slide.

V.
R.P. really dug into that cement: here are the deep grooves
of an act of will aged fifty years,
of imposing oneself on the unyielding universe.
Tacked his nobody initials
to some nobody monument man and left
questions hanging in the air
like cartoon thought-bubbles—at the very least,

he was here.

Socrates Goes to a House Party

I. Who Let This Socrates Bitch into the House Party

No, I don't know

what the gods want. My cup is full

of pride and hubris, a caustic warmth

in my belly. I imagine

I was split off from something in the beginning:

another person, a floor of clouds,

a bright gold sound.

And this is why i'm stupid and smoking

like it's a part-time job,

just something before my photography takes off,

you know? Hey, you're not so bad

Socrates. You're ugly and you ask too many questions,

but you're not so bad.

II. Oh Shit, Socrates Died at the House Party

Cover the body in a white sheet

but not before we mistake his stillness for sleep:

death in sunglasses, death on the floor,

death with a sharpie-covered face. We're not heathens,

just very far from what's sacred.

We feel closest to the gods when we're stumbling,

half-blind, prophet by the sea:

Run through the woods and fall for a beautiful deer.

Your children will be half-spirit

and not belong anywhere.

Tin Can to God

God is tired of lambs and flapping lips. God is tired of blood—
it stains his hem and it's a real bore to get it out. He's tired of
other people speaking for him, but the way things are set up, he
has to use a tin can and a long, long string to reach us, and only
one person can listen to the other side at a time. Today God is
asking for the things no one has thought to give him: cigarette
butts, bits of glass, earbuds with the innards ripped out, green
pennies, gray wads of gum, matchbox cars missing their wheels.
Things he's never gotten his hands on, all the little intimacies
passed between palms and then sent flying through car
windows, lost out of pockets, discarded at dusk. I don't know
what he plans to do with them, but that's God for you—he
speaks in mustard seeds and similes that bend like light around
his brow. The streetlights sigh and come alive—moths run
headlong into the warmth. A few boys kick a can down the
street. God sits at his kitchen table, a single bulb above. He
counts his pennies.

housework

good that living takes so much maintenance. the dishes go in
the cupboard go on the table go in the sink go back in the
cupboard and i go to bed go to the grocery store go to the
bank go to your house go to my house go to bed. how else
would i spend my time if not putting on, casting off. tides of
television, flickering lights, coffee maker, dirty cup. i am
happy to be full of small tasks. silverware in my fists now in
the drawer. peeling off a bit of skin behind my ear. we need
more orange juice, bread, milk. in the spring, the work goes
outdoors: grass and gardens, removing sticks, digging ourselves
out of inches of snow. in the middle of the mundane, miracles
peeking through the concrete: clover caught in my hair,
perfectly smooth rock, beetle husk. i'm bringing them home to
you. for the first time i want to sit and do nothing. this is a
small task: holding your body to mine, my nose in your hair,
the whole night unfurling outside the window.

We Wake Up and Go Looking

We wake up and go looking for cathedral ceilings
underneath benches, in coffee cups,
in the nearest mouth,
moving the tongue aside to find
empty tabernacles, a singular fly drowsing out.
We imagine falling upwards until we burn,
reverse-meteorites, pulled
by our throat-cords into the sky.

We wake up and we're forgetting
something important,
the name of the lake we visited once
with someone we loved.
We're afraid we'll wander for forty years and still
not have our helping of milk and honey.
We want to take our time
studying someone's face, but they turn away

so quickly—next stop, next aisle, next
person. We must be looking
for something to invest in:
a nest in a ribcage, a hole in the ground, a stomach
in the hands of a man in the sky.

Burning down, falling up.
We grab at what we can, whether it's clouds or hands
or pieces of scrap metal.
We're not sure what we're searching for but we feel
closer to it when we take a stranger's
hand, show him the way
to the well.
The earth just barely holds our heels.

About the Author

Kimberly Ramos is a queer Filipina writer from Missouri, though they currently reside in Providence, Rhode Island, as a graduate student of philosophy at Brown University. When not studying (or avoiding studying), they serve as the Managing Editor of CLASH!, an Imprint of Mouthfeel Press. They dream of becoming a cryptid and haunting the Midwest. You can read more of their work at kimramoswrites.carrd.com

About the Press

Unsolicited Press is based out of Portland, Oregon and focuses on the works of the unsung and underrepresented. As a womxn-owned, all-volunteer small publisher that doesn't worry about profits as much as championing exceptional literature, we have the privilege of partnering with authors skirting the fringes of the lit world. We've worked with emerging and award-winning authors such as Shann Ray, Amy Shimshon-Santo, Brook Bhagat, Kris Amos, and John W. Bateman.

Learn more at unsolicitedpress.com. Find us on twitter and instagram.